JOKE BOOK

TRY NOT TO LAUGH

12 YEAR OLD EDITION

D0861093

CHALLENGE™

Copyright© 2019 by Try Not to Laugh Challenge Joke Group

ALL RIGHTS RESERVED. By purchase of this book, you have been licensed one copy
for personal use only. No part of this work may be reproduced, redistributed, or
used in any form or by any means without prior written permission of the
publisher and copyright owner.

Try Not To Laugh Challenge
BONUS PLAY

Join our Joke Club and get the Bonus Play PDF!

Simply send us an email to:

TNTLPublishing@gmail.com

and you will get the following:

- 10 Hilarious, Bonus Jokes
- An entry in our Monthly Giveaway of a $50 Amazon Gift card!

We draw a new winner each month and will contact you via email!

Good luck!

WELCOME TO THE
TRY NOT TO LAUGH CHALLENGE!

RULES OF THE GAME:

★ Grab a friend or family member, a pen/pencil, and your comedic skills! Determine who will be "Jokester 1" and "Jokester 2".

★ Take turns reading the jokes aloud to each other, and check the box next to each joke you get a laugh from! Each laugh box is worth 1 point, and the pages are labeled to instruct and guide when it is each player's turn.

★ Once you have both completed telling jokes in the round, tally up your laugh points and mark it down on each score page! There is a total of 10 Rounds.

★ Play as many rounds as you like! Once you reach the last round, Round 10, tally up ALL points from the previous rounds to determine who is the CHAMPION LAUGH MASTER!

★ Round 11 - The Tie-Breaker Round.

In the event of a tie, proceed to Round 11. This round will be 'Winner Takes All!', so whoever scores more laugh points in this round alone, is crowned the CHAMPION LAUGH MASTER!

TIP: Use an expressive voice, facial expressions, and even silly body movement to really get the most out of each joke and keep the crowd laughing!

Now, it's time to play!

ROUND 1

What do you call a farming accident?

A COW-tastrophe!

☐ LAUGH

What did the robber say at the Zoo?

"Take the bunny and run!"

☐ LAUGH

What is hummus' favorite Disney character?

PITA Pan!

☐ LAUGH

What do you call a bedroom furniture delivery service?

Bed-Ex!

☐ LAUGH

Did you hear about the scheming farmer?

He was plotting his revenge.

LAUGH

What should a good artist do while camping?

Leave no trace...

LAUGH

Why is there an empty spot in the Periodic Table?

So there is always room for the element of surprise!

LAUGH

Why did the vacuum quit?

His job SUCKED and he was tired of being PUSHED around!

LAUGH

Pass the book to Jokester 2! ➡

How do you teach a steam engine a new trick?

You TRAIN it.

LAUGH ▢

What do you call it when a really skinny person visits Hawaii?

A TOO WEAK vacation!

LAUGH ▢

I went to the Grand Canyon when it was foggy. I just wish I could see the HOLE thing.

LAUGH ▢

Why don't subtraction problems get along?

They have their DIFFERENCES.

LAUGH ▢

 **JOKESTER 2**

What did one horse say to the other?

"Can I ask you equestrian?"

LAUGH

Why did the bear get chosen for the job?

No one really knows. He just has a certain KOALA-ty.

LAUGH

Who is a leopard's favorite singer?

Mick JAGUAR!

LAUGH

What do you call a displeased hippo?

Dis-HIPPO-inted!

LAUGH

Time to add up your points! →

SCORE BOARD

Add up each Jokester's laugh points
for this round!

JOKESTER 1

$\dfrac{\quad\quad}{\text{Total}}$ **/8**

JOKESTER 2

$\dfrac{\quad\quad}{\text{Total}}$ **/8**

ROUND WINNER

ROUND
2

Why are gifts bad at remembering?

They're always living in the PRESENT!

☐ LAUGH

What did the apple say to the juice?

"You're my main squeeze!"

☐ LAUGH

How do they make calls in jail?

With a CELL phone!

☐ LAUGH

Why didn't the potato play poker?

It didn't have any chips!

☐ LAUGH

Did you hear about the woman who was indifferent to singing?

She didn't CARE-aoke.

LAUGH

What's a surgeon's favorite instrument?

The organ.

LAUGH

What photo filter will make you look bigger in the winter?

'The Snowball Effect.'

LAUGH

What do you call a mummy's business plan?

A Pyramid Scheme.

LAUGH

Pass the book to Jokester 2! ➔

What did the grape say to the raisin?

"Have you lost weight?"

LAUGH

What mushroom can you land a plane on?

The Air-Portabella!

LAUGH

Why did the piece of bread look both ways?

It was CROISSANT the street!

LAUGH

The beef doesn't like to lose. There's too much at steak.

LAUGH

What did the camera say to the lens?

"I always pictured us together."

☐ LAUGH

Why did the turn signal and the steering wheel break-up?

They had an on-again, off-again relationship.

☐ LAUGH

Why are circles overqualified for most jobs?

They have so many degrees!

☐ LAUGH

What did 5 and 3 tell the other numbers, when they asked them to dinner?

"It's okay. We 8."

☐ LAUGH

Time to add up your points! →

SCORE BOARD

Add up each Jokester's laugh points for this round!

JOKESTER 1

/8

Total

JOKESTER 2

/8

Total

ROUND WINNER

ROUND

3

Where did Aspirin get its healing abilities from?

It's Auntie Biotics. (Antibiotics)

LAUGH ☐

What happens to trains when they die?

E-terminal Slumber.

LAUGH ☐

Which organization meets on fairways?

Golf Clubs.

LAUGH ☐

What type of food do you eat during a yoga class?

Medi-Tator Tots.

LAUGH ☐

JOKESTER 1

What does Nutella do before getting on a sandwich?

It gets b-READY!

LAUGH ☐

Why does the jigsaw puzzle enjoy getting put together?

Because then it's at PIECE with itself.

LAUGH ☐

What does the Minister say when watering his crops?

"Lettuce spray!"

LAUGH ☐

Why are meteorologists so rich?

Every cloud has a silver lining!

LAUGH ☐

Pass the book to Jokester 2! ➝

How do you pick up a car, in the dark of night, while staying warm?

A light, jack it.

 LAUGH

Why is it so hard to dance with horses?

They always think you MUSTANG-o!

 LAUGH

What's a comedian's favorite candy bar?

Snickers!

LAUGH

How long do nocturnal birds sleep?

OWL day!

 LAUGH

24

How do ghosts listen to music?

With a BOO-mbox!

☐ LAUGH

Researchers just found a 70-foot electric guitar submerged under water in Scotland.
Their suspicions were confirmed.
The Rock-Ness Monster does exist!

☐ LAUGH

Why does no one understand what the shrub really wants?

Because it's always beating around the bush!

 LAUGH

Who is Australia's #1 superhero?

Wom-Bat Man!

 LAUGH

Time to add up your points! ➝

SCORE BOARD

Add up each Jokester's laugh points for this round!

JOKESTER 1  $\dfrac{}{\text{Total}}$ /8

JOKESTER 2 $\dfrac{}{\text{Total}}$ /8

ROUND WINNER

ROUND

4

Who is Genghis Khan's favorite football team?

The Raiders.

LAUGH

Why did the yogi put a bowl of cereal on her head?

For a BALANCED breakfast.

LAUGH

Why did the collector quit his job?

It was taxing!

LAUGH

I have a friend, Shay, whose last name is Kitoff. Well, whenever she was in doubt, she would just Shay Kitoff!

LAUGH

Why did the boy wake up thinking he was a policeman?

He had a BADGE dream!

☐ LAUGH

How do you cheer up an angry fish stick?

Dip it in some HAR-HAR sauce!

☐ LAUGH

There was a sneaky bug watching me in my room one night. I found out it was just a foreign SPY-der.

☐ LAUGH

Why did the woman fill her parka with pine needles?

She wanted a FIR coat!

☐ LAUGH

Pass the book to Jokester 2! ➞

 **JOKESTER 2**

How do reptiles ask each other to dinner?

"I-guana take you out to eat!"

 LAUGH

How do cows listen to music in their cars?

With an OX cord!

 LAUGH

What do you call a strong lion's grip?

A MANE squeeze!

 LAUGH

What is a snake's favorite musical?

MAMBA Mia!

 LAUGH

 **JOKESTER 2**

Music Teacher: "Sally, did your mother write you a note?"
Sally: "No, ma'am. She can't read music."

LAUGH

I have many degrees, but I have never been to college. What am I?

A Thermometer!

LAUGH

Why was the money so sad?

It was all a-LOAN!

LAUGH

What is a lock's favorite type of clothing?

Kha-KEYS!

LAUGH

Time to add up your points! →

SCORE BOARD

Add up each Jokester's laugh points for this round!

JOKESTER 1   /8
                  ‾‾‾‾‾‾
                   Total

JOKESTER 2   /8
                  ‾‾‾‾‾‾
                   Total

ROUND WINNER

ROUND
5

Teacher: "Josie, why are birds so important?"
Josie: "They came up with the first Tweet!"

LAUGH

Why was the milk so fast?

It would always run right past-eur-ize.

LAUGH

What country ate the most food in 2019?

SNACK-istan.

LAUGH

What kind of meat does one person like to eat?

SOLO-mi.

LAUGH

Where can you find 100 feet in less than an inch?

On a centipede!

LAUGH

Where should wheels be muddy, spinning, and going nowhere?

A pottery studio!

LAUGH

In what family are the babies considered 'daddy's'?

A family of Daddy Long Legs!

LAUGH

What kind of dress does a mattress look best in?

A Spring Dress!

LAUGH

Pass the book to Jokester 2! ➔

What famous American loved the earth?

Recycling BIN-jamin Franklin!

LAUGH

What do you call a backpack you put on backwards?

A packback!

LAUGH

Why is it so expensive to keep papers together?

You have to PAY-per clip!

LAUGH

What subject lets you find emotions anywhere in the world?

Geograph-Feelings!

LAUGH

 **JOKESTER 2**

Why did the pony borrow money?

He was a bit SHORT.

◯ LAUGH

Why do birds love tennis so much?

TOU-CAN play together!

◯ LAUGH

Why was the rabbit so apathetic?

He didn't CARROT all!

◯ LAUGH

What happens when you go to sleep during an earthquake?

You wake up on the wrong side of the bed!

◯ LAUGH

Time to add up your points! ➡

SCORE BOARD

Add up each Jokester's laugh points for this round!

JOKESTER 1

$$\frac{}{\text{Total}} \quad /8$$

JOKESTER 2

$$\frac{}{\text{Total}} \quad /8$$

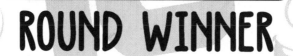

ROUND WINNER

ROUND 6

What do you call a pulsating heart?

A heartthrob.

◻ LAUGH

Why did the farmer think his lambs had run away?

He hadn't HERD them in a while,
but they were just being a little SHEEPISH.

◻ LAUGH

Do you know why I always pay with cash, instead of a credit card?

I just like to use my common cents.

◻ LAUGH

What did the broken hangglider say?

"GLIDE rather not."

◻ LAUGH

Whose Marty Mcfly's favorite rapper?

Future.

☐ LAUGH

Why was Dracula fired?

He sucked at his job.

☐ LAUGH

When do pizza men work the hardest?

When they really knead the dough!

☐ LAUGH

What do you call a critical grandmother?

A knit-picker.

☐ LAUGH

Pass the book to Jokester 2! ➜

What kind of hat gives the best math advice?

Add-VISOR!

☐ LAUGH

What did the sailor say when the boy asked if he knew lashings?

"I do knot."

☐ LAUGH

Do you who is the single best smeller in the world?

There are a lot of contenders, so I guess no one NOSE.

☐ LAUGH

Where does cheese learn the alphabet?

BRIE-school.

☐ LAUGH

What's it like being a bison?

It has its buffa-highs and buffa-lows.

LAUGH

What do you call a
correct author?

A righter! (Writer)

LAUGH

'Round and 'round and around
they go, nothing above and
nothing below, always on
track, they race through the
black, but the one that can't
run, sure can glow!

What am I?

LAUGH

The Solar System!

What do you call a lost wolf?

Where wolf?!

Time to add up your points! →

LAUGH

SCORE BOARD

Add up each Jokester's laugh points
for this round!

JOKESTER 1

$\dfrac{}{\text{Total}}$ /8

JOKESTER 2

$\dfrac{}{\text{Total}}$ /8

ROUND WINNER

ROUND

7

What do you call clams on a ship?

Ahoy-sters!

○ LAUGH

What bug likes pillows and blankets?

Bedbugs.

○ LAUGH

Why do librarians blow things out of proportion?

They tend to OVERDUE things.

○ LAUGH

Why couldn't the electrician get his tulips to sprout?

He planted the wrong kind of bulbs!

○ LAUGH

What rodent is the most religious?

A chip-MONK!

 LAUGH

Why did the sports fan throw carrots and potatoes to one side of the field?

He wanted to show which team he ROOTS for.

LAUGH

What do you call an entrance, a big cow, and a cutie?

A door, a bull...

LAUGH

How do well dressed people make money?

In vests.

LAUGH

Pass the book to Jokester 2! →

Why was the geometry teacher said to be unfocused?

He kept going off on TANGENTS!

◻ LAUGH

What does President Clinton like to play in his spare time?

BILL-iards!

◻ LAUGH

What do you call a baseball built out of money?

A FARE ball!

◻ LAUGH

What city in New Mexico is said to be the fastest?

Gallup.

◻ LAUGH

 **JOKESTER 2**

Why are people who grow herbs so successful?

Well, you know what they say, THYME is money!

◻ LAUGH

What is a business man's favorite cuisine?

TIE food!

◻ LAUGH

Why didn't the boy want to play the board game?

He thought it seemed a bit DICEY.

◻ LAUGH

My friend kept bugging me about going rock climbing... I told him to take a hike!

◻ LAUGH

Time to add up your points! →

SCORE BOARD

Add up each Jokester's laugh points
for this round!

JOKESTER 1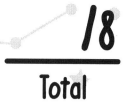

$$\frac{}{\text{Total}} /8$$

JOKESTER 2

$$\frac{}{\text{Total}} /8$$

ROUND WINNER

ROUND

8

The surgeon is always asking me about life. He really likes picking my brain.

LAUGH

Why did the boy take his grandmother to the mountains on her birthday?

Because she was as old as the hills!

LAUGH

Why don't people like to sing in a group at first?

It's an a-CHOIR-ed taste.

LAUGH

Why was the multiplication shop so successful?

They were always coming out with new PRODUCTS!

LAUGH

How did Caesar travel the world?

He just ROME-d around!

☐ LAUGH

Should you read music when you're tired?

Yes, because there are lots of RESTS.

☐ LAUGH

How is the man who lives with cheetahs doing?

SAFARI hasn't gotten eaten!

☐ LAUGH

Why did the guitarist stop playing after becoming a lawyer?

He wanted to rest his case!

☐ LAUGH

Pass the book to Jokester 2! ➝

Why do birds work out so much?

To get big PECKS.

LAUGH

What do numbers and cattle have in common?

They can both be rounded up!

LAUGH

I'm fast and strong, but my four legs are round. When I first wake up, I like to make a big sound! I only start moving when someone's around, and I only like running on certain types of ground. What am I?

A Car!

LAUGH

Why was the elevator the MVP?

It worked hard on every level!

LAUGH

 **JOKESTER 2**

What kind of rating does our solar system have on Amazon?

One star.

LAUGH ☐

What do birds wear to formal events?

Sweater Nests.

LAUGH ☐

Why do moles like living underground?

It's WORM and cozy!

LAUGH ☐

What camera equipment does an amateur photographer use?

TRY-pods.

LAUGH ☐

Time to add up your points! ➡

SCORE BOARD

Add up each Jokester's laugh points for this round!

JOKESTER 1

$$\frac{\qquad}{\text{Total}} \quad /8$$

JOKESTER 2

$$\frac{\qquad}{\text{Total}} \quad /8$$

ROUND WINNER

ROUND
9

Where did the pig go to take a nap?

His HAM-mock!

LAUGH

How do French ghosts say 'Thank you'?

"Merci BOO-coup!"

LAUGH

Why shouldn't you work-out with spiders?

Every day is leg day!

LAUGH

Why did the astronaut break-up with her boyfriend?

She needed some SPACE.

LAUGH

 **JOKESTER 1**

Where are the biggest banks in the U.S. located?
Along the Great Lakes!
○ LAUGH

How many insects can live in a building?
Ten-ants.
○ LAUGH

Why do seaside towns have a lot of things plugged into them?
Because of all the ports!
○ LAUGH

Why was the ostrich such a great performer?
He was very EMU-sing!
○ LAUGH

Pass the book to Jokester 2! →

What did the skeleton say to the doctor?

"I don't have the heart to go on anymore."

LAUGH

What do you call a tangled rope on a boat?

KNOT-ical.

LAUGH

What did the police yell to the square thief?

"We've got you cornered!"

LAUGH

I find that walking is actually the least tiring way to get around the city. Public transportation really takes a TOLL.

LAUGH

 **JOKESTER 2**

While driving my dad to work, he asked me to put on some cartoons. I responded with, "How? We're in the car!?" and he said, "Yeah, I said put on some CAR TUNES!"

☐ LAUGH

Why do knitter's eat so fast?

They're always SCARF-ing down their food!

☐ LAUGH

How does pepper fly so cheap?

He waits for the seasonal deals!

☐ LAUGH

What do dermatologists say, when getting rid of pimples?

"It'll be gone in a pinch."

☐ LAUGH

Time to add up your points! ➜

SCORE BOARD

Add up each Jokester's laugh points for this round!

JOKESTER 1

/8
—————
Total

JOKESTER 2

/8
—————
Total

ROUND WINNER

ROUND
10

 **JOKESTER 1**

How did the pirate convince the judges he should win first place at the Art Fair?

He drew his sword.

LAUGH

Why did the musicians get in trouble during class?

They were passing notes!

LAUGH

What did the lightbulb say to the lamp?

"Socket to me!"

LAUGH

What should you do with a suspicious fence door?

Investi-GATE.

LAUGH

64

 **JOKESTER 1**

Knock Knock.
Who's there?
Hummus.
Hummus, who?
Hummus song, it will cheer
you up!

 LAUGH

What set belongs to
everybody and nobody at
the same time?

The sunset!

LAUGH

What is useless until it
gets blown up?

An inflatable raft!

LAUGH

What's a tree's favorite highway?

ROOT 66!

Pass the book to Jokester 2! LAUGH

Which hand on the clock is the most generous?

The h-OUR hand.

LAUGH

Why was the pilot disappointed, when he got his brand new jet?

Turns out, it was just a little plane.

LAUGH

What did the sweater say when it got a snag?

"Feels like I'm unraveling! Guess life isn't always what it SEAMS..."

LAUGH

What happens when a wall is impressed?

It gets floored!

LAUGH

What do you call it when twins travel the world together?
A world TWO-er! (Tour)

☐ LAUGH

What sport does James Bond play?
SPY-ke ball!

☐ LAUGH

Knock Knock.
Who's there?
Slate.
Slate, who?
Slate to be out on the porch!
Let me in!

☐ LAUGH

Where do ants go to find their relatives?
ANT-cestry.com!

☐ LAUGH

Time to add up your points! ➡

SCORE BOARD

Add up each Jokester's laugh points for this round!

JOKESTER 1

/8
Total

JOKESTER 2

/8
Total

ROUND WINNER

Add up all your points from each round.
The Jokester with the most points is crowned
The Laugh Master!
In the event of a tie, continue to Round 11
- The Tie-Breaker Round!

JOKESTER 1 _____
Grand Total

JOKESTER 2 _____
Grand Total

_____
THE LAUGH MASTER

ROUND

11

TIE-BREAKER
(Winner Takes ALL!)

What do you call it when the hot and cold faucets turn on at the same time?

Kitchen SYNC.

○ LAUGH

Who is the librarian's favorite band?

Quiet Riot.

○ LAUGH

What do you call a dry cleaner who gives you compliments?

A Self-esteamer!

○ LAUGH

Who does yoga and cuts down trees all day?

A LIMBER-jack!

○ LAUGH

 **JOKESTER 1**

What did the cyclops say to the other cyclops?

"I've got an EYE for you!"

◻ LAUGH

Why are artichokes considered the sweetest vegetable?

Because they have big HEARTS.

◻ LAUGH

What do you call a Mexican dish that's been poked?

Holey-Molé!

◻ LAUGH

Why did the wheel no longer work?

It was re-TIRED!

◻ LAUGH

Pass the book to Jokester 2! ➜

What did the chicken go to college for?

EGG-counting.

☐ LAUGH

What do a tire and a candle have in common?

They both get blown out sometimes!

☐ LAUGH

What's George Washington's favorite movie?

Independence Day.

☐ LAUGH

What do you call a young drummer?

A Baby Boomer.

☐ LAUGH

74

Why did the hotel clerk give the man a candy bar?

He had asked for a suite!

☐ LAUGH

What do you do if the door on your bird cage breaks?

You re-PARROT!

☐ LAUGH

What's the best way to get around a new town?

With a Jeep.P.S.

☐ LAUGH

I'm getting really good at making hot beverages. I got it down to a TEA.

☐ LAUGH

Time to add up your points! →

Add up all your points from the
Tie-Breaker Round.
The Jokester with the most points is crowned

The Laugh Master!

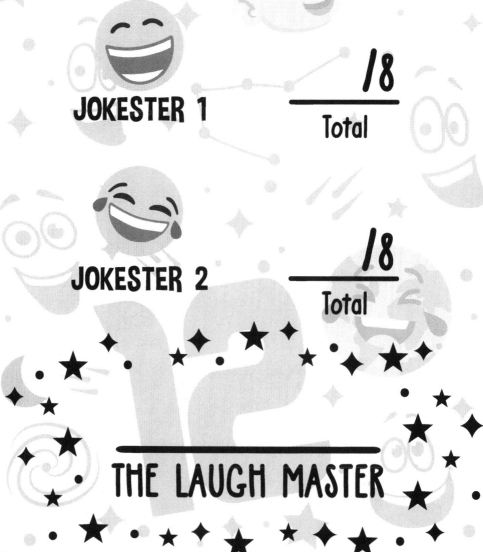

JOKESTER 1 /8
_____
Total

JOKESTER 2 /8
_____
Total

_____
THE LAUGH MASTER

Check out our

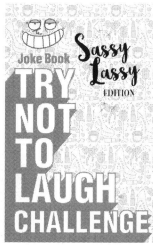

Visit our Amazon Store at:

other joke books!

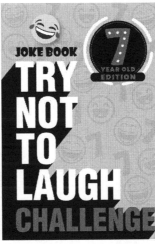

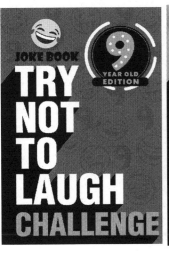
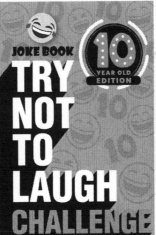
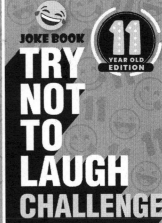

www.Amazon.com/author/CrazyCorey

Made in the USA
Columbia, SC
18 November 2019

83294081R00046